# How to Make Money on ODesk

## Brian Ford

# Table of Content

Introduction

Why ODesk

Creating an ODesk Account

Making the Account Buyer Friendly

Finding Your Jobs

How to Bid Properly

Conclusion

# Introduction

Do you want to be a freelancer? If you want to be a freelancer then you have to come to ODesk for jobs.

ODesk is the largest marketplace on this earth that can give you your desired jobs. There are lots of other marketplaces which offer tons of jobs too but the main difference of ODesk with those other sites is, ODesk is the most professional site among all these sites. When you are dealing with money, you always want to work on a dependable platform. ODesk is exactly that platform for you.

ODesk started its journey is 2003. It is a global platform and you can use this platform to earn from wherever you want. It doesn't matter whether you are from USA or from a third world country, you can get equal opportunities to earn from ODesk and that is why ODesk is special.

Before we dig into the deep ocean of outsourcing and setting up a killing account, you should have a clear idea on outsourcing. Firstly, outsourcing is the same jobs that people used to do at their offices. Now these jobs are done online at a cheaper rate and at a quicker time. Also, the world is getting digitalized and that is why new jobs and market sectors are building up. These sectors need freelancers  and that is the booster of outsourcing. Let's look at two examples.

Previously an architect  used to go to his office and work on his designs after getting a project.

He couldn't generally get a project from another country but now with the help of ODesk, the architect can get easy jobs from another country and do that sitting at his or her home.

Also, digital industries such as kindle of Amazon or news based websites around the world are becoming popular. These websites need to be built up; these websites need contents, they need to be maintained. All these works can be done via hiring freelancers and there is no better place to hire freelancers than ODesk in this current world.

This book will describe you every detail that you need to know to start making money from ODesk. Remember, this book will not teach you job skills, this book will talk about all the skills and other details that you need to know to build up a professional profile. It can be said that if you are dedicated and hardworking then you will be able to start earning money after finishing this book. Everything is written in easy and clear words. Hopefully you will be benefited.

# Why ODesk

If you are interested in earning money as a freelancer then ODesk is a great place for you. Even if someone asks why ODesk is better than other freelancing sites then this chapter will be the answer. Let's discuss why ODesk is better and why you should select ODesk and only ODesk.

- ODesk is the only quality job place where there are jobs for each and every skills. No matter what skill you do have, you will get jobs for your skill on ODesk. There are other marketplaces where you will only get jobs as a designer or as a writer; ODesk is free from that problem. It is a big community and you will get jobs for any skill that you have.

- When you are choosing marketplaces to work, you should be careful about their professionalism. ODesk is highly professional and their support team along live support system is always active. Your problems will be solved at a quicker time here than in any other places.

- ODesk gives guaranty in hourly payments. There is quality snapshot software of ODesk which helps them to count how many hours a freelancer is working. They release payment on every Monday on those hours and this payment is guaranteed. Apart from their Monday payments of hourly jobs, ODesk also allow freelancers to take fixed jobs. You will hardly get cheated on ODesk because of their super management system.

- The rating system of ODesk is professional. It is not only the buyers who will give you ratings; you will also be able to give ratings to the buyers. You can also complain about fake or false ratings if you want to change or delete them.

- ODesk will alert you to stop the work if your buyer does not have enough money to his or her ODesk wallet. In this way, you will never end up working extra.

- ODesk allows you to search jobs according to your skills. There are thousands of jobs being posted each day on ODesk but you will only see those jobs that you want to see. Also, ODesk updates the jobs live time which means that you will immediately be able to see new jobs when they are posted.

- The payment method of ODesk is easy to handle and wide. You can take your earned money either via wire transfer, via paypal or moneybookers and also via some other methods. Receiving your earned money was never this much easier before.

- ODesk takes only 10% of your earnings from a job and they take it after you are done with the job and the payment. It will never happen that ODesk will take the money before you. They only take the money if you are paid properly, otherwise they won't take the money.

These are the most important benefits of ODesk and these are the reasons that why you should select ODesk to start your freelancing career. Thousands of freelancers are starting their journey on ODesk every day and most of them who have skills are earning a lot of money. Why won't you be one of them?

# Creating an ODesk Account

In this chapter, we will discuss how to create an ODesk account. Things will be discussed in details and it will be easy for you to create an account on ODesk. Let's start the journey.

The first thing that you need before creating an ODesk account is an internet connection and a computer. You can create an account from your mobile but it will be impossible for you to do freelancing from your mobile. That is why PC is a pre-required thing.

If you do not have an email id then the first task is to create an email account. It is easy to create an email id and we will not discuss that in this chapter. Let's start creating an ODesk account. Firstly, go to www.ODesk.com. Now you have to click on 'looking for a job' or similar lines from the home page. ODesk keeps changing this line but you will find a similar line in the main page which is basically the sign up page.

After you are done with clicking on the sign up link, you will be headed towards the sign up page. Fill up all the information that is asked in this page. Make sure that you are giving true information because ODesk may verify your account later and if your information is not true then they will have the rights to suspend your account. If you are unsure about information then keep that blank and proceed.

After you click on the submit button, you will get a confirmation email in your email account which will have the ODesk id and password of your choice.

Do not start bidding on jobs. You need to work on your profile now. The first task is to give a profile picture. Make sure that your profile picture is a smart and smiling one.

You don't need to give a passport size photo of you where you are wearing suits. Just make sure that you are smiling in your profile picture. A smiley face is always believable and buyers love them.

After you are done with your profile picture, it is time to write your profile review. Again, you don't have to be very professional and you don't have to use tough languages here. The profile review is a review of what you do. This is the first thing that buyers will see when they will come to your profile. That is why it is important to have a quality profile review. Tell what you do, why do you love to do that and tell about your experiences. Also, make sure that your profile overview has a quality title. The title is the most important thing in your profile. The title should tell about your dedication and also about your job skills. Research a bit and check other profiles before you write your title. Do not copy anyone, be smart and find a new one.

In your profile, you have to fill up certain sections such as certification, experience, and portfolio. You should never ever think that this information is not important. All these information will play major roles in getting your first job. Getting your first few jobs will be tough and you need to make your profile 100% perfect to make sure that you have better chances of getting jobs.

If you do not have certificates then do not come up with a fake one. Keep that place blank. If you don't have experience then tries to have some experiences before applying to your desired jobs. Also, if you don't have a portfolio then make sure that you create one. Creating a portfolio is not a difficult task. It will be discussed in the next chapter.

# Making the Account Buyer Friendly

Buyer friendly account does not mean something very tough or hard and fast. It is basically portraying a positive image of yours to the buyers. Almost in all the cases, buyers will visit your profile before awarding you the job. Also, there can be cases where buyers will post jobs and will send invitations to some freelancers who have good profile according to the buyers. If you can achieve that invitation then it will be working as an extra benefit for you in getting that job. This is why having a buyer friendly account is so important.

How can you make your account buyer friendly? The first way is by creating a killer portfolio. Portfolio is the most important tool of impressing a buyer. See, it is not tough to understand why your portfolio is so important. Buyers will hire you for a certain job and to know about your skills, they will always visit your portfolio section. If they like it then they will hire you, if they don't like it then they won't hire you. It is that simple. Now, how to make a good portfolio?

The current trend is to have a portfolio website where you will display all your works. If you don't have one or do not want to make one then there is nothing to worry. You can showcase your portfolio in your profile section. As you are reading this book, it can be assumed that you have certain skills already to apply for jobs. For example, let's think that you are a web developer and you create websites. Now, before creating an id on ODesk, you must have created websites. If your website is live then take that url and put it in a word file. Now write about your site and how you created it. If it is not live then take a .zip folder and put your website in it and also put a separate file on how you created it. Always try to give three to four portfolio files. If you work on something small in size (for example logo making) then create one portfolio with 10-

20 samples in it. Also mention which software you use to create logo and those details. Details of your portfolio are as important as your main work. Always make sure that you write details about your portfolio.

Apart from the portfolio, buyers also look at some other details of your profile. They never bother about your username or age. Buyers are never biased and they try to pick the best one for their job. The second thing that you should put importance on is the hourly rate. Remember, the hourly rate that you put on your profile is not the final one. You can change that while you are bidding but even then that hourly rate has a major role to play. When buyers will visit your profile, they will check that to find out how demanding you are. If you want to work as an eBook writer and your profile hourly rate is $50/hour then you will never get hired. Again, if it $1 per hour then also you will find it hard to get jobs. The best idea is to study some similar profiles before setting up your own one.

We already discussed the overview part and it won't be discussed again but the overview is also important.

You should keep one thing in mind that no matter what you write, you should be able to justify that. You cannot just write that you are the best web developer of this world. You have to have justifications for that. Try to mix humbleness, honesty and skills in your write-ups. Buyers do not only look for skilled workers, they want people who can maintain deadlines, who are honest and who are hard working. Make sure that these things are being portrayed in your profile details.

ODesk is always trying to come up with new facilities for promoting your profile. Their latest facility is to publish a video record of around 1 minute in your profile. The old freelancers are not aware of this new feature and you can take that advantage if you want. Turn your camera on and tell about yourself. Do not start telling about your family or schooling, tell about your skills, tell about your honesty and punctuality. Tell the buyers why they should hire you and finish the video with a smile. A smiling face can do wonders; you can prove that with your video.

# Finding your jobs

Finding your job is one of the most important parts of the whole ODesk project. If you cannot find your desired job then there is no point in setting up the whole profile with good words, commitments and skills. Finding the first job is one of the toughest tasks in ODesk. As you do not have any prior experience or ratings to show, it becomes tough to impress the buyers. This is why you need to be patient and active at the same time to get your first job.

First thing that you need to do to get your first job is proper time management. There is a non-written rule in ODesk that whoever bids in a job first holds better chances of winning that job. You don't have to be the first one every time but try to be in top five. That will work for you as an advantage. Bidding and writing your cover letter is the most important part and in most cases this is the decider of whether you will get the job or not. The next chapter will discuss everything about that.

If you do set your skills properly then you will be able to find your desired jobs in the 'find jobs' section. You will not see jobs from all the categories here. You have to select your desired category from the left section of your screen. Also, if you want to get some special types of jobs then there is a search bar on the top of the find job page. For example, you work as a writer but you do not want to check all the writing related jobs, you are only interested in eBooks. Simply search eBook writing on the search bar and you will get your desired result. You can also save that searching and from the next time you will get this search result whenever you want.

# How to Bid properly

Bidding is one of the key parts of getting a job. If you cannot bid properly then your whole work will go in vain. You will never be able to get your desired job without a proper bid with a cover letter. Bidding is the last hurdle of getting a job. In this chapter, we will discuss everything about how you can bid and win a job.

Firstly, click on your desired job and open that job. Before reading to the job description, the first task is to find out how many people already completed their bid before you. This is important because if more than 10 people have already bid on a job, you should not bid there. Yes, if you do not find other appropriate jobs for you then try to look at these things. Do those old bids have good profile? Did the buyer say that he or she will hire more than 1 freelancer? If the answers are positive then you can apply to this job. Otherwise, start searching for new jobs.

Now, the first task after opening a job is to read that job perfectly. You should never ever do spam bids. ODesk is very serious about spam bids and they can suspend your account if they find out that you are doing spam bids. Now-a-days buyers know that they will get spam bids in their job postings and that is why they do a little trick in their job description. You will find them saying that you should start your bid with a special word. If you do not start with that special word, buyers will ignore your bid. This is why you should read the job description very carefully before bidding.

Now, after you are done reading the job post, you should think whether you will be able to meet the demand of your buyer or not. If you are confident that you will be able to satisfy him or her with your work then proceed, otherwise look for a new job. Do not bid to those jobs that you are not sure of finishing perfectly. Do not bid on to jobs that you are 50% sure of completing. Also, do not think that you will learn how to do the job after you get it. You have to learn it first and then you should apply to the job.

Before applying to the job, check about the buyer's budget. When you will click on 'apply', you will find an option where you can write your desired amount. Now, make sure that your asking amount is not too low or too high. It should be a smart one. Then there is an option of asking for upfront payment. You should always ask for 25-50% upfront for jobs. If buyers do not agree to give you upfront then ask them to give you milestones. After you are done with this milestone part you have to write the cover letter which is the place to impress your buyer.

If it is an hourly job then write the amount that you want to get for each hour. It is not necessary to go with your profile hourly rate. You can make a new one for this job.

Start with writing your experiences which will help you to do this job. Tell the buyer that how long you will take to finish this job and tell how you are going to do that. If possible then tell the buyer that you are going to update him or her regularly about the job. If it is a writing related job then promise that you will never plagiarize and there will never be grammar error in your work. If it is designs based work then tell your buyer that you will give him all the formats and the buyer will have the rights. Make sure that there is no grammar error or spelling error in your cover letter. Poor grammar will show that you are not serious about the job. If you're English is not so good then take help from a friend of yours to get this cover letter done.

After you are done writing the cover letter, it is time to attach your best possible sample which will go with this job. Do not just add random samples with the cover letter. Think before you attach and try to attach similar kind of work samples. That will help a lot.

After you attach the sample, it is time to recheck the whole thing. Remember that you should not take hours to bid on to a job.

You have to make it fast so that your bid is placed above others. After you confirm that everything is perfect, press on bid. There will be a pop up window where you will have to reconfirm the bid and after checking that, you are done.

Now it is time to wait for the reply of buyers. Remember, buyers do not want to wait too long. Try to keep your email messenger on because whenever a buyer will knock you, you will get an email in your mailbox. Try to give them replies as soon as you can. This will bring positive impression about you to them.

After you finish the job, the formal way of submitting the work is via 'my jobs' section. Go there and click on send message. Write that the job is done on the subject field and attach your work there. Also, if you want then you can simply attach the work in reply of the previous messages. There is no problem with that.

After you deliver the job, it is time for your buyer to check it. Be helpful and stay on your toes. A bad review from your buyer can ruin the whole profile. Try to satisfy them.

Satisfying doesn't mean that you have to do extra work or something, if the buyer threatens you then tell ODesk about this issue. They will solve it for you.

After the buyer ends the job, you will give him/her a review and he will do the same. When both reviews will be published, ODesk will take around 24 hours to make them available. That's it. Your first job is done.

# Conclusion

When you are working on ODesk, make sure that you never cheat. ODesk is very serious regarding their policies. You may think that they won't understand but actually they will.

ODesk even blocks internet protocol (IP) addresses if they find out that you are cheating with your work. If you are working on an hourly job, do not ever think that you can ask one of your friends to do it for you on a day. It will harm you for sure.

When you will complete your first job, you will find the path of ODesk easier than before. It will continue to be easier and easier. You have to be patient to get your first job and when you get it, make sure that you give your best in it. Also, if you cannot do a work after taking it, simply return all the money of the buyer and tell them sorry. Your profile will be safe in this way. Maintaining your profile is a key thing and you have to be careful about it.

If you can make everything right then it is sure that you will be earning soon from ODesk. ODesk has a great live support system. Ask them anything whenever you need. They are helpful and will help you in your problems.

Best of Luck.